Muffins to Slim By

Muffins to Slim By

Fast Low-Carb Gluten-Free Bread & Muffin Recipes to Mix & Microwave in a Mug

By

Em Elless

Book and Cover Design by M.L. Smith

MUFN Books™

MUFN Books™

Table of Contents

Muffins to Slim By

Author Introduction

My goal in writing *Muffins to Slim By* has been to share innovative recipes that are not only gluten-free and low in carbohydrates, but that take low-carb breads to new highs in variety, nutrition and taste satisfaction. There is no "diet" here. The food is too delicious and gratifying. Which sounds better to eat, highly processed wheat flour paste (what it turns to inside our bodies) or nutritious almonds milled into a soft, fine meal? Finely ground coconut flour with its heavenly tropical aroma, high in fiber and protein - or starchy white flour stripped and bleached of everything useful? Once you taste the difference you will never want anything else.

Although I have been creating recipes for over forty years, it wasn't until my doctor told me that I was borderline diabetic that I learned that low-fat diets were too high in fat – on my body! Numerous research studies showed that refined carbs are the major culprit - foods robbed of everything but starches and sugars and commonly processed (again!) into most foods we eat.

But there is such a thing as too many "good" carbs, too. Carbohydrates quickly convert to sugar in the bloodstream and the higher the blood glucose, the more insulin the body needs to process the sugar. *Insulin is the fat storing hormone*! Even for non-diabetics, excess carbs pile on the pounds. Just one slice of whole grain bread has 14 carbs – half my entire daily allowance! But a hamburger wrapped in a lettuce leaf, no bun? Tuna salad trowelled into a celery stalk, but no sandwich? No way! Not for very long, anyway.

I needed to make serious lifestyle changes, but it was difficult and time consuming finding products that didn't have hidden sugars or that relied heavily on refined white flours. Those that worked were expensive and limited in choice. So my quest for creating low-carb muffins began, with an emphasis on a wide variety of delicious, nutrient-rich foods.

I rely primarily on plant foods, non-starchy vegetables, nuts, berries, fish, poultry, eggs and dairy products. They provide thousands of micronutrients, antioxidants, vitamins, minerals, and fiber that protect against chronic disease, which I highlight throughout this book. These "super foods" have also contributed to significant weight loss! Protein foods (meat, cheese and eggs) and fats (such as butter and oils) have no or very few carbohydrates. I do allow myself occasional servings of whole-grain pasta, or a baked or sweet potato, but these are only occasional. Hydrogenated oils, sugar and white flour remain off-limits.

Regardless of the particular low-carb or gluten-free program you are following, you will find many bread choices that will fit into your eating plan, some that will work even for those in the starting phases of their plan (like the Atkins Induction). The concept of "minute" muffins is not new, and many wonderful recipes can be found online and in some diet plans, but every recipe in *Muffins to Slim By* is an original creation, tasted and re-tasted until the "This is it!' moment. Most are much larger than regular-sized muffins and make a filling breakfast, packed with protein and fiber. Add a salad and you will have a satisfying meal.

So banish any thought of deprivation in your weight loss goals. Preparing healthful recipes is one of the most satisfying, rewarding things we can do for ourselves. You will discover the most delicious muffins you have ever tasted - anywhere! Many are actually fun to put together, and unbelievably fast. Each is a gift to yourself - but you will want to share them!

Em Elless

Cookware, Techniques & Ingredients

3" Wide - Inside

4" High

Approximate size of
Mug should be:
4" High by 3" Wide
Approximate size of
Ramekin should be:
2" High by 4" Across

4" Across - Inside Measure

2" High - Inside Measure

Microwaves: The cooking power/watts and behavior of your own microwave most likely varies from mine, so the cooking time listed is approximate. The rule of thumb for doneness you will see throughout is, "when top springs back when pressed." It doesn't hurt the muffin to start checking it 15 seconds before the time I list, and rechecking every 10-15 seconds.

....

❖ Almost all the recipes are mixed with a spoon and microwaved in the same dish; no prior spraying with cooking oil is required.

❖ Baking Powder has a tendency to clump so smash it smooth before baking.

❖ The muffin will pop out (sometimes a little nudge with a knife or spoon is needed) if you immediately transfer it to a saucer, top-side up. The bottom will be moist for a few seconds.

❖ Occasionally air pockets develop on the bottom of the muffin when they are baked in a mug. They quickly disappear when you eat them. : <)

When you first go low carb, one of the first things you discover is that some of the ingredients you need are not readily available locally. Many gluten-free flours - potato, rice, and tapioca flour - are even higher in carbohydrates than wheat flour. I recommend Netrition online for most of your low carb needs. I've also found good deals for the flours on Amazon.

I decided not to use any prepackaged mixes in my recipes as they are easy to put together, are much less expensive and give you control over the quality of all your ingredients. Brands vary, and you will develop your own favorites. These will become your new staples.

Note on Nutrition/Carb Information: The calculations I list with each recipe are based on standard products I use which are readily available. It is important to read labels and compare brands! The difference you will find in carbs, fiber, sugars, "fillers" etc. can vary widely and thus your carb totals may differ.

....

Flaxseed Meal/Ground Flaxseed: The chewy seeds, which many call one of the most powerful foods on the planet, are packed with omega-3 fatty acids, antioxidants, fiber, minerals, and essential vitamins. There are two types of flaxseed meal: brown and golden. The brown flaxseed is less expensive than the golden, but the nutritional benefits are the same. You can also buy the seed in bulk and grind it yourself with a blender or coffee grinder. Most nutrition experts recommend ground flaxseed because your body is better able to digest its vital nutrients.

Coconut flour is naturally 75% fiber in composition, containing 9-10 grams per two tablespoons, which reduces the absorption of sugar into the blood stream. It is produced from grinding the dried white internal meat of the coconut. It has significant protein content and a low glycemic index, which means it will satisfy your hunger longer.

Almond Flour: Because it is simply ground almonds, it offers the same health benefits as eating them whole – rich in vitamins and minerals, high in protein and fiber. Some almond flours are more coarsely ground, which dictates the texture. I prefer the very fine mill and baking results using JK Gourmet Almond Flour.

Soy Flour is a high-protein, calcium-rich flour produced by grinding roasted soybeans. It adds fine texture, tenderness and moistness to baked goods. In addition to the excellent nutritional value of soy protein, scientists have found that consumption of soy protein can contribute to reducing LDL "bad" cholesterol and the risk of heart disease, plus cancer-fighting is flavones.

Whey Protein is a complete protein, which means it contains all the amino acids our bodies must absorb from food without adding fat, carbs or significant calories. Brands vary widely so be sure to read labels! I use *Market Pantry Vanilla Whey Protein* purchased at Target. The vanilla flavoring adds creamy flavor and the sugar content is less than half a carb in most recipes.

Stevia/Sweetener: Many artificial sweeteners and "sugar free" products on the market contain fillers such as dextrose or maltodextrin. These can raise blood sugar just as much as real sugar. I prefer 100% stevia powders. The brand I use is Kal. I also prefer EZ-Sweetz drops as it seems to me to have the least bitter aftertaste but you should use your favorite brand. Each brand has a different unit of measuring: teaspoons, drops, a packet, or a tiny scoop. In this book, wherever a "serving" of stevia is mentioned, this means "equal to the sweetness of 1 teaspoon of sugar."

Canned Pumpkin improves the texture, color and adds moisture to baked goods. Don't be afraid to try it when you see it as an ingredient in a non-pumpkin muffin recipe - you cannot taste the pumpkin! Sour cream or whipped cream cheese may be substituted. The color and texture will be affected and may be more "eggy" or spongy, but I like them either way. Do not buy the *pumpkin pie filling*! Make sure that the only ingredient is pumpkin.

Sour Cream/Whipped Cream Cheese is used in many of the muffin recipes as a replacement for oils. Yes, they are high in fats (which is why it is a good replacement) but compare the difference if you were using oils:

In <u>2 tablespoons of sour cream</u> there are: 50 calories; 4.5 g total fat; 2.5 g saturated fat, and; 2 carbs.
In <u>2 tablespoons of canola oil</u> there are: 240 calories; 30 grams total fat; 2 g saturated fat, 0 carbs.

There is considerable debate on the pros and cons of saturated fats, with many experts agreeing that refined carbs pose a much greater danger. I believe that moderation is the key, but avoid refined sugar and hydrogenated oils whenever possible. Margarine is one of the worst things we can eat.

 Introducing New Fruit Substitutes

The Italians call it "melanzane," which means "crazy apple." I call it "mock fruit." The flesh is spongy and bland and has the wonderful ability to absorb surrounding flavors, mocking any fruit we choose. Originally it looked like goose eggs so the name "eggplant" stuck, even after centuries of hybridizing into colorful new shapes and sizes.

Although we think of eggplant as a vegetable usually breaded and fried and covered in cheese, it is botanically classified as a berry. And as my cooking experiments have discovered, this versatile fruit can be substituted for those that are very high in carbohydrates: bananas, apples, peaches, pineapple, etc. It can be incorporated in countless ways in all our low-carb cooking. Whether in muffins or stir-fry, it is impossible to detect from the real thing.

The most common variety is pear shaped with glossy, dark-purple skin and spongy, cream-colored flesh. Contained within the bulbous portion are small, sesame-sized seeds arranged in a circular pattern. Early varieties were very bitter to the taste and required a salting process to purge the bitterness, but cultivation and crossbreeding have greatly improved the flavor. While some cooks use the salting process before frying eggplant to reduce oil absorption, for our purpose that is exactly what we want it to do.

Choose heavy, firm fruit with unblemished skin. If the flesh gives slightly when you gently press with your thumb, then bounces back, it is ripe. If the impression remains, it is overripe and not suitable. If it is too hard to press (if you can actually knock on it!), it was picked too early. Eggplant can be blanched or steamed, then frozen for up to six months. The only way eggplant is unacceptable is raw. I prefer it peeled for fruit preparation, but for other dishes I leave the skin on. The skin of purple eggplants contains a powerful antioxidant called nasunin, found in many richly colored vegetables and berries. The small seeds are edible and add interesting texture.

Eggplant Nutrition Facts (1 cup cooked, cubed)
Calories 27.7 (*¼ cup per muffin recipe = 7 calories*)
Protein .82 gram
Carbohydrates 6.57 grams (¼ cup = 1.6 net carbs)
Dietary Fiber 2.48 grams
Potassium 245.52 mg

Equivalents
1 medium eggplant = about 1 1/2 pounds
1 pound = 4 cups, diced
1 pound fresh = 1-3/4 cups, cooked and cubed

To Freeze
Wash, peel if desired, and slice 1/3-inch thick. Water blanch, covered, for 4 minutes in one gallon boiling water containing 1/2 cup lemon juice (fresh or bottled). Cool, drain and seal in zip closure freezer bags.

Flavorings
There are many wonderful fruit-flavored extracts on the market. The brand I use for the apple, pineapple and peach flavors is *LorAnn super-strength*, along with their *Tart and Sour Flavor Boost* to give fruits like apple and pineapple the convincing tang they require. For sweetener I prefer *EZ-Sweetz liquid* as it seems to me to have the least bitter aftertaste. But whatever liquid brand is your personal favorite will work fine.

Cooking Directions
Put canola oil, fruit flavoring/s, liquid sweetener and food coloring per each recipe in microwave-safe container and stir until liquids are blended. Add peeled, diced eggplant and stir until each piece is coated with flavored oil. Microwave 1 minute and stir contents. Microwave 1 additional minute. Remove and stir. You now have 1/2 cup of cooked fruit, enough for 2 muffin recipes. You can double the recipe and freeze ¼ cup portions for future baking. I wrap mine in clear plastic wrap and put the bundles in a labeled zip-lock freezer bag. (Note: I make all my favorite fruits from the same eggplant in about half an hour and freeze the little bundles for later (except one for immediate use!).

FRUIT SUBSTITUTES

Apples

1 rounded Cup peeled, diced
eggplant
1 T **canola oil**
10 drops **EZ-Sweetz** (or liquid
sweetener equal to 10 tsp.)
1 tsp. **LorAnn Apple** Flavor
8 drops **LorAnn Tart and Sour
Flavor Boost**
1 tsp. **cinnamon** (optional)

Pineapple

1 rounded Cup peeled, diced
eggplant
1 T **canola oil**
10-12 drops **EZ-Sweetz** (or
liquid equal to 10-12 tsp.)
1 tsp. **LorAnn Peach** flavor
10 drops **LorAnn Tart and Sour
Flavor Boost**
yellow food coloring

Peaches

1 rounded Cup peeled, diced
eggplant
1 T **canola oil**
10 drops **EZ Sweetz** (or liquid
sweetener to equal 10 tsp.)
1 tsp. **LorAnn Peach** Flavor
yellow/orange food coloring

Bananas

1 rounded Cup peeled, diced
eggplant
1 T **canola oil**
10 drops EZ Sweetz (or liquid
sweetener to equal 10 tsp.)
1 ½ tsp. **banana extract**
yellow food coloring

Measurements

¼ tsp. = 15 drops

½ tsp. = 30 drops

1 tsp. = 1/3 T or 60 drops

3 tsp. = 1

½ T = 1 ½ tsp.

1 T = 3 tsp.

2 T = 1/8 cup

16 T = 1 cup

1/8 cup = 2 T

¼ cup = 4 T

1/3 cup = 5 T + 1 t

3/8 cup = ¼ cup + 2 T

½ cup = 8 T

¾ Cup = 12 T

2/3 cup = 10 T + 2 tsp. 1 cup = 16 T

BAKING MIXES

Having baking mixes on hand will allow you to prepare, bake and enjoy muffins in less than five minutes – lifesavers when you're tired, hungry and in a hurry!

Baking Mix One: Makes 8 Recipes

1 C   **almond flour**
2/3 C **vanilla whey protein**
1/3 C **coconut flour** (5T + 1 tsp.)
1 tsp.   **salt**
2 T   * **baking powder**
2 ½ T **stevia or equivalent**

* Press baking powder through a strainer. It has a strong tendency to clump and will show up in small white clusters in your finished muffin.

Mix well and store in air-tight container.

Single Serving Ingredients

2 T **almond flour**   *3 g protein; 3 g carbs; 1.5 g fiber = 1.5 net carbs*
1 T **vanilla whey protein**   *4 g protein; <1 g carb*
1 T **coconut flour** *<1 g protein; 2.7 g carbs; 1.7 g fiber = 1 g net carb*
1/8 tsp. (dash) **salt**
2/3 tsp. **baking powder**
1 tsp. **stevia or equivalent**

Baking Mix Two: Makes 8 Recipes

1 C **flaxseed meal**
½ C **almond flour**
½ C **coconut flour**
1 tsp. **salt**
2 T ***baking powder**
2 ½ T (8 tsp.) **stevia**

* Press baking powder through a strainer. It has a strong tendency to clump and will show up in small white clusters in your finished muffin.

Mix well and store in air-tight container.

Single Serving Ingredients:

2 T **flaxseed meal**   *3 g protein; 4 g carbs; 4 g fiber = 0 net carbs*
1 T **almond flour** *1.5 g protein; 1.5 g carbs; .75 g fiber = .75 net carbs*
1 T **coconut flour** *1 g protein; 4 g carbs; 2.5 g fiber = 1.5 g net carbs*
1/8 tsp. (dash) **salt**
2/3 tsp. **baking powder**
1 tsp. **stevia or equivalent**

Sweet Muffins

You will want to cuddle up with this dreamy pillow every chance you get. It is deeply satisfying, warm and wonderful with a delicious tang.

√Lemons are a great natural remedy to improve your health, with strong immune-boosting powers, antioxidents and their use as a weight loss aid.

•

260 calories; 10 g protein; 4.8. g total carbs – 1.5 g fiber = 3.3 net carbs

Lemon Cream Cheese Pillow

¼ C **whipped cream cheese**
1 T **lemon juice**
1 **egg**
6 drops **EZ-Sweetz** (or equivalent
to 2 T **sweetener**)
1 T **almond flour**
1 tsp. **coconut flour**
1 tsp. **baking powder**
Dash of **salt**

In ramekin or mug: Soften cream cheese in microwave a few seconds.

Add lemon juice, egg and sweetener and mix well.

Add dry ingredients and blend well.

Microwave 1 minute 45 seconds – 2 minutes, or until top springs back when pressed.

Cranberry Sauce

12 oz. bag of fresh **cranberries**
1 C **water**
Sweetener equal to 1 C of sugar, *or*
  ¾ C *sugar-free pineapple syrup and reduce water to ¼ C
Pinch of **salt**

* Sugar-free strawberry, raspberry, apple syrups also work well.

Bring to boil and cook 5-10 minutes until thickened.

A 12 oz. bag of fresh cranberries contains 3 cups, with a total of 150 calories, 12 g fiber, 36 carbs = 24 net carbs.

√Cranberries outrank nearly every fruit and vegetable--including strawberries, broccoli, spinach, red grapes, raspberries, and cherries in disease-fighting anti-oxidents. But their health benefits are almost totally removed when large amounts of sugar is added. So for pure goodness and health benefits, enjoy this sugar-free recipe.

165 calories; 9 g protein; 6.5 g total carbs; 3. 5 g fiber = 3.5 net carbs

Cranberry Orange Muffin

1 **egg**
1 T **coconut flour**
1 T **almond flour**
1 T **sour cream** or **plain whole yogurt**
*4 tsp. **sugar free cranberry sauce** (see recipe opposite page)
1 tsp. **baking powder**
1/2 tsp. **orange extract**
2 servings **sweetener** (equivalent to 2 tsp. of sugar)

Combine all ingredients except cranberry sauce in a mug and mix well.

Swirl in cranberry sauce – *do not mix completely.*

Microwave on high approximately 70 seconds.

Invert immediately onto a plate and enjoy.

*Option: For a delicious **Plain Orange-Flavored Muffin**, omit cranberry sauce.

R ichly satisfying! **Pumpkin** adds moisture and leaves behind no flavor when used in small amounts. It is a good staple to have on hand for all your reduced-oil baking.

√New studies show that flavonoid-rich *pure cocoa* prepared without less desirable ingredients (sugar, corn syrup, hydrogenated oils, etc.) has been associated with decreased blood pressure and improvement in cholesterol levels, among other benefits.

150 calories; 9 g protein; 10 total carbs; 4.2 g fiber = 5.8 g net carbs

 # Red Velvet

1 **egg**
1 T **coconut flour**
2 T **canned pumpkin**
1 T **sour cream**
1 T **cocoa**
2 drops **EZ-Sweetz** (or equivalent to 2 tsp.)
1 tsp. **baking powder**
½ - ¾ tsp. **LorAnn Red Velvet Bakery Emulsion**

Stir all ingredients in mug or ramekin until well blended.

Microwave approximately 1 minute, or until top springs back when pressed.

Spread with sweetened whipped cream cheese, if desired.

Pecans are very rich sources of several important B-complex groups of vitamins such as riboflavin, niacin, thiamin, pantothenic acid, vitamin B-6, and folates.

√Research from the USDA shows that pecans rank among the top 15 foods with the highest levels of antioxidants.

307 calories; 13 g protein; 13 g total carbs; -8 g fiber = 5 net carbs

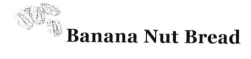 **Banana Nut Bread**

1/4 C **Baking Mix Two**, or:

> 2 T **flaxseed meal**
> 1 T **almond flour**
> 1 T **coconut flour**
> 1/8 tsp. (dash) **salt**
> 2/3 tsp. **baking powder**
> 1 tsp. **stevia or equivalent**

½ tsp. **banana flavoring**, _or_ ¼ C **banana fruit substitute**
1 drop **EZ-Sweetz** or sweetener equal to 1 tsp.
2 T **sour cream**
1 **egg**
1/2 tsp. **butter flavor**
1 T chopped **pecans**

Mix all ingredients in mug or ramekin. Microwave for 2 minutes if banana flavoring is used. **NOTE**: _Microwave 2 ½ minutes if banana fruit substitute is used._

Early Spanish explorers called it coco, which means "monkey face" because the three indentations (eyes) on the hairy nut resembles the head and face of a monkey.

√**Because of its strong antioxidant properties and health benefits, coconuts can be used to lower cholesterol, regulate hormones, stabilize glucose levels, fight off viruses, increase metabolism and fight infections, among many other life-improving qualities.**

315 calories; 12 g protein; 9.5 g total carbs; 3.5 g fiber = 6 net carbs

Coconut Cream Muffin

1/4 C **Baking Mix One**, *or*:

> 2 T   **almond flour**
> 4 tsp.   (1 T + 1 tsp.) **vanilla whey protein**
> 2 tsp.   **coconut flour**
> 1/8 tsp. (dash) **salt**
> 2/3 tsp. **baking powder**
> 1 tsp. **stevia or equivalent**

2 T **unsweetened coconut**
2 T **sour cream**
3 drops **EZ-Sweetz** or equal
   to 3 tsp. sweetener
½ tsp. **vanilla**
1 **egg**

Combine all ingredients in mug or ramekin and mix with spoon.
Microwave 1 minute 15 seconds, or until top springs back when pressed.

I call this recipe "Sugar Buster" because several studies suggest that **cinnamon** has a regulatory effect on blood sugar, making it especially beneficial for hypoglycemics and people with Type 2 diabetes – in addition to being great for weight loss.

√The potential health benefits attributable to cinnamon can be stated as nothing short of astonishing. 1/2 teaspoon per day can lower your bad cholesterol (or LDL).

125 calories; 5 g protein; 7 g total carbs; 5 g fiber = 2 net carbs

Cinnamon Sugar-Buster Muffin

2 T **flaxseed meal**
1 T **almond flour**
1 tsp. **cinnamon**
1 tsp. **baking powder**
2 tsp. **stevia**
½ tsp. **vanilla**
1 T **sour cream**
1 **egg**
dash of **salt**

Combine all ingredients in mug and mix until well blended.

Microwave 50 seconds to 1 minute, or until top springs back when pressed.

So many health benefits in one fast, fantastic muffin!

My **eggplant** substitute for pineapple contains a potent antioxidant called nasunin in addition to numerous B-vitamins, vitamin C, proteins, minerals and potassium.

√The National Diabetes Education Program, Mayo Clinic and American Diabetes Association recommend an eggplant based diet as a choice for management of type 2 diabetes due to its high fiber and low soluble carbohydrate content.

297 calories; 14 g protein; 11 g total carbs; 3.2 g fiber = 7.8 net carbs

Pineapple Upside-Down Cake

¼ C **pineapple fruit substitute**, *room temperature*
¼ C **Baking Mix One,** *or*

> 2 T   **almond flour**
> 4 tsp.   (1 T + 1 tsp.) **vanilla whey protein**
> 2 tsp.   **coconut flour**
> 1/8 tsp. (dash) **salt**
> 2/3 tsp. **baking powder**
> 1 tsp. **stevia or equivalent**

1 **egg**
1 T **butter**
1 tsp. **vanilla**
1 tsp. **maple flavor**
½ tsp. **coffee extract**
½ tsp. **caramel flavor**
9 drops **EZ-Sweetz** (or liquid sweeter equal to 1 T)

Melt butter in ramekin 30 seconds. Add all flavorings and sweetener and stir until liquids are blended.   Arrange pineapple evenly across bottom of ramekin.
In separate dish, thoroughly blend Baking Mix and egg.
Drop batter by spoonsful onto fruit.
Microwave 1 minute 30 seconds, or until top springs back when pressed. Place saucer on ramekin (use hotpads!) and turn upside down, so that pineapple will be on top when you lift off ramekin.
Top with whipped cream, if desired. So-o-o Delicious!

Pumpkins are incredibly rich in vital antioxidants, vitamins, minerals and other healthy nutrients. They owe their bright orange color to a high amount of carotenoids, which assist in staving off free radicals in the body and help in preventing premature aging, cardiovascular diseases and other infections.

√ **Pumpkin seeds are a rich source of protein. One ounce of pumpkin seeds contains approx. 7 grams of protein. Their oil is high in phytosterols which can replace cholesterol in the body and help in reducing the blood cholesterol levels.**

Recipe makes 2 ample servings:

Per Muffin: 175 calories; 7.4 g protein; 7 g total carbs; 3 g fiber = 4 net carbs

*Pumpkin Nut Muffin

¼ C **canned pumpkin**
2 T **sour cream**
1 **egg**
1 tsp. **rum or vanilla extract**
2 drops **EZ Sweetz** (or sweetener equivalent to 2 tsp.)
1 tsp. **baking powder**
¼ C **almond flour**
1 T finely chopped **pecans**

In mug or ramekin: Blend pumpkin, sweetener, egg, extract and sour cream.

Add dry ingredients and pecans and blend well.

Microwave approx. 2 ½ minutes (test at 2 minutes by pressing top lightly to see if it is dry and springs back).

Invert onto plate, slice and butter halves, if desired.

*Makes 2 ample servings.

Coconut flour is a delicious fine white meal produced from grinding the dried white internal meat of the coconut. It contains almost double the amount of fiber found in wheat bran – giving it the highest level of fiber on the flour market - . but is completely gluten free.

√ **The high fiber content of coconut flour is fermentable and produces high amounts of butyric acid, which is a cancer fighter. Lab studies have shown that it can slow the growth of tumor cells and promotes normal cell development. Coconut fiber not only removes carcinogenic toxins, it helps prevent conditions that promote cancer.**

270 calories; 15 g protein; 7.5 g total carbs; 3.2 g fiber = 4.3 net carbs

Melt-in-Your-Mouth Muffin (With Option)

¼ C **Baking Mix One**, *or*

       2 T **almond flour**
       4 tsp. (1 T + 1 tsp.) **vanilla whey protein**
       2 tsp. **coconut flour**
       1/8 tsp. (dash) **salt**
       2/3 tsp. **baking powder**
       1 tsp. **stevia or equivalent**

1 **egg**
2 T **sour cream** *or* **whipped cream cheese**, softened
½ tsp. **vanilla extract**

In large mug or ramekin: Mix all ingredients until well blended.

Microwave 1 ½ or 2 minutes, or until top springs back when pressed.

OPTION: When you are really, really in a hurry and want a basic, fast muffin, just mix ¼ cup Baking Mix (either One or Two) with 1 egg and 1 T of sour cream or yogurt, whip it up and microwave for a minute and a half.

Pure cocoa is associated with decreased blood pressure and improvement in cholesterol levels, among other benefits. The darker chocolate with the most concentrated cocoa will be the most beneficial.

√**Sugar free dark chocolate is rich in flavonoids (antioxidants) and has been linked to reductions in risk factors for diabetes.**

*Like many of my muffin recipes, this makes 2 regular size or 1 very large muffin.

Large: 345 calories; 17 g protein; 12.7 g total carbs; 4.2 g fiber = 8.5 net carbs
Regular: 173 calories; 8.5 g protein; 6.35 g total carbs; 2.1 g fiber = 4.25 net carbs

 ***Chocolate Muffin**

1/4 C **Baking Mix One**, *or*:

> 2 T **almond flour**
> 4 tsp. (1 T + 1 tsp.) **vanilla whey protein**
> 2 tsp. **coconut flour**
> 1/8 tsp. (dash) **salt**
> 2/3 tsp. **baking powder**
> 1 tsp. **stevia or equivalent**

1/4 C **whipped cream cheese**
1 T **cocoa**
3 drops **EZ-Sweetz (or equal to 1 T sweetener)**
1 **egg**
1/2 tsp. **vanilla**

Soften cream cheese a few seconds in microwave. Add all other ingredients and blend well.

Microwave 1 ½ minutes, or until top springs back when pressed.

*Makes 2 regular-size muffins.

Zucchini is a very low-calorie vegetable, with only 17 calories per 100 g. All parts of summer squash are edible, including the flesh, seeds and skin. For those who steam and freeze surplus vegetables for later use, findings show that even previously frozen zucchini maintains its antioxidant benefits fairly well.

√Zucchini is a very strong source of key antioxidant nutrients, including the carotenoids lutein and zeaxanthin. Since the skin of this food is particularly antioxidant-rich, it's worth leaving the skin intact.

295 calories; 14.5 g protein; 12 g total carbs; 8.25 g fiber = 3.75 net carbs

 **Zucchini Muffin**

1/4 C **sour cream**
1/4 C (slightly rounded) shredded **zucchini**
1 **egg**
1/4 C **flaxseed meal**
1 tsp. **baking powder**
1 tsp. **cinnamon**
2 tsp **stevia** (or 2 drops EZ-Sweetz)
dash of **salt**

In cup or ramekin: Blend sour cream, zucchini and egg.
Add flax meal, baking powder, cinnamon, stevia and salt, mixing well.
Microwave 2 minutes, or until top springs back when pressed.
A moist, delicious, nutritious muffin!

Coconuts were used extensively in the Pacific during World War II. Since blood plasma supplies were scarce, it was common for medics to siphon pure coconut water from young coconuts to be used as emergency plasma transfusions for soldiers who were injured. "It (coconut juice) is considered a close substitute for blood plasma since it is sterile, cool, easily absorbed by the body and does not destroy red blood cells. To quote Morton Satin, Chief of the United Nations Food and Agriculture Organization: "It is a natural isotonic beverage with the same level of electrolytic balance as we have in our blood. It is the fluid of life, so to speak."

√Among its growing list of benefits, coconuts have been shown to: improve digestion; ward off wrinkles; build cells; increase thyroid production; aid weight loss; increase metabolism; kill bacteria.

* Makes 1 very large or 2 regular muffins.
1 Regular: 163 calories; 7.7 g protein; 5.7 g total carbs; 2 g fiber = 3.7 net carbs

 ***Piná Colada Muffin**

1/4 C **Baking Mix One**, *or*

> 2 T   **almond flour**
> 4 tsp.   (1 T + 1 tsp.) **vanilla whey protein**
> 2 tsp.   **coconut flour**
> 1/8 tsp. (dash) **salt**
> 2/3 tsp. **baking powder**
> 1 tsp. **stevia or equivalent**

1 **egg**
2 T **whipped cream cheese,** warmed
1 T **unsweetened coconut**
1 tsp. **rum extract**
2 drops **EZ Sweetz** (or sweetener equivalent to 2 tsp.)
1/4 C **pineapple fruit substitute**

Set out pineapple fruit substitute to bring to room temperature.
Combine all ingredients in large mug or ramekin.
Microwave 2 minutes, or until top springs back when pressed.
Cool slightly and top with whipped cream (optional).

*Makes 2 ample servings.

Cinnamon has been shown in studies to reduce cytokines linked to arthritic pain.
Flaxseed Meal is a mega source for the plant version of omega-3, called alpha-linolenic acid.
Almond flour is high in magnesium, calcium, fiber, B-vitamins, Vitamin E, and healthy fat!

√**Grain-based flours are primarily carbohydrates. Almond, Flaxseed and Coconut flours are gluten-free, low in carbohydrates, high in fiber and a high source of protein.**

With sour cream:
Large: 257 calories; 12.5 g protein; 12 g total carbs; 7.5 g fiber = 4.5 net carbs
Regular Size: 129 calories; 6.25 g protein; 6 g total carbs; 3.8 g fiber = 2.25 net carbs

*Cinnamon Apple/Fruit Muffin

¼ C **Baking Mix Two**, *or*

> 2 T **flaxseed meal**
> 1 T **almond flour**
> 1 T **coconut flour**
> 1/8 tsp. (dash) **salt**
> 2/3 tsp. **baking powder**
> 1 tsp. **stevia or equivalent**

1 **egg**
2 T **sour cream** (optional)
1/4 C **fruit substitute of your choice**

Bring fruit substitute to room temperature.
Mix all ingredients well in 4" ramekin.
Microwave: *Without* sour cream: 1 ½ minutes +
                    With sour cream: 2 - 2½ minutes +
     +or until top springs back when pressed.

Wonderful and moist, with ample fruit throughout, delicious spread with butter.

*Makes 2 ample servings

Lemons contain 22 anti-cancer compounds including limonene, an oil which slows or halts the growth of cancer tumors in animals and flavonol glycosides, which stop cancer cell division.

√**Health benefits of lemon include treatment of throat infections, indigestion, fever, kidney stones, skin care, rheumatism, and high blood pressure.**

210 calories; 10.75 g protein; 7.75 total carbs; 4 g fiber = 3.75 net carbs

# Lemon Poppy Seed

1 **egg**
1 packet **True Lemon***
2 tsp. **coconut flour**
2 T **almond flour**
1 T **sour cream** *or* **plain whole yogurt**
1 tsp. **baking powder**
1 tsp. **poppy seeds**
3 servings **sweetener** (or equal to 3 tsp. sugar)

In a mug, combine dry ingredients.
Add egg, sour cream or yogurt and mix well. Let sit at least 30 seconds, then stir again.
Microwave approximately 1 minute, or until top springs back when pressed.
Invert immediately onto a plate and enjoy!

***NOTE**: 1 ½ T concentrated lemon juice can be substituted for the True Lemon, but if you use this, *increase the coconut flour to 1 T.*

OPTION: For a delicious **Lime Muffin**, follow the recipe above, but simply substitute a packet of True Lime for the True Lemon and omit the poppy seeds.

Some call **flaxseed** one of the most powerful plant foods on earth. While it is not technically a grain, it has a similar vitamin and mineral profile to grains. But the high amount of fiber, antioxidants, and Omega-3 fatty acids in flax leaves grains far behind.

√Omega-3 Fatty Acids are a key force against inflammation in our bodies. Mounting evidence shows that inflammation plays a major role in many chronic diseases including arthritis, heart disease, diabetes, asthma, and some cancers.

170 calories; 9.75 g protein; 6 g total carbs; 3 g fiber = 3 g net carbs

Toffee/Butterscotch Muffin

1 **egg**
1 T **flaxseed meal**
1 T **almond flour**
1 T **sour cream** *or* **plain yogurt**
1 T canned **pumpkin** (flavor disappears, adds moistness)
1 tsp. **baking powder**
2 drops **EZ-Sweetz** (or sweetener equal to 2 tsp.)
*15 drops **English Toffee** (*or* **Butterscotch**) **Candy Oil**
        (I use LorAnn Brand)

Blend egg, sour cream (or yogurt) and pumpkin in mug or ramekin.

Add remaining ingredients and mix together.

Microwave approx. 1 minute 15 seconds, or until top springs back when pressed.

*Option: For a delicious **orange-flavored muffin**, substitute ½ tsp.
Orange extract.

Peanuts (and avocados) are unfortunately too often placed on many people's bad-for-you lists for their high fat content. But researchers have discovered that this type of fat is the mono-unsaturated kind that is extremely good for our hearts and our overall health.

√**Peanuts are packed with many important B-complex groups of vitamins such as riboflavin, niacin, thiamin, pantothenic acid, vitamin B-6, and folates. They are also an excellent source of vitamin E (a-tocopherol).**

With cream cheese and chocolate:
241 calories; 12.75 g protein; 8.5 g total carbs; 4 g fiber = 4.5 net carbs
Without cream cheese and chocolate:
190 calories; 11.5 g protein; 6 g total carbs; 3 g fiber = 3 net carbs

Peanut Butter/Peanut Butter Chocolate Chip

    1 T **flaxseed meal**
    2 T **peanut butter**, room temperature
    3 drops **EZ-Sweetz** (or equal to 1 T)
    1 tsp. **baking powder**
    1 **egg**
    1 T **whipped cream cheese** *or* **sour cream** (optional)
    ½ tsp**. peanut butter flavor** (optional)
    1 T finely chopped **dark chocolate** (optional)

Combine peanut butter, cream cheese (or sour cream), egg, sweetener and optional flavoring until egg is well blended into peanut butter.
Mix in flaxseed meal and baking powder.
Stir in chocolate bits, if desired.
Microwave 1 minute, or until top springs back when pressed.

This is a meal in itself.

NOTE ON PEANUT BUTTER: Many brands have added sugars and oils. Check the label and buy a brand with peanuts only, or peanuts and salt – or buy freshly ground – YUM!

With three grams of fiber per one-cup serving, **pumpkin** can keep you feeling full longer with only 49 calories. It is extremely effective for treating gastrointestinal disorders and also helps in lowering the LDL (bad) cholesterol levels in the blood and in regulating blood sugar levels.

√Pumpkin is a storehouse of potassium and Zinc. Studies show that eating a potassium-rich diet can prevent the onset of cardiovascular diseases and hypertension. Zinc is important in the maintenance of bone density.

120 calories; 8 g protein; 9 g total carbs; 4.5 g fiber = 4.5 net carbs

 **Pumpkin Spice**

1 **egg**
1 T **coconut flour**
3 T **canned pumpkin**
¼ tsp. **vanilla extract**
1 tsp. **baking powder**
1 tsp. **pumpkin pie spice**
2 tsp. **stevia** or equivalent sweetener

In mug, mix egg, pumpkin and vanilla until well blended.

Add coconut flour, baking powder, spice and sweetener and mix until completely blended.

Microwave approximately 1 minute 20 seconds or until top midway to center springs back when pressed.

NOTE: Center of top may be slightly damp but it dries in a few seconds.

Wonderful served with butter or whipped cream cheese.

Pumpkin is one of the food items recommended by dieticians in cholesterol controlling and weight reduction programs. Pumpkins are natural diuretics, which help flush toxins and unwanted waste from the body.

√Pumpkins are high in Lutein & Zeaxanthin which protect the eyes against free radical damage and prevent formation of cataracts and degeneration of the eye tissues. The high amount of Vitamin A, C and E will help give you healthy, glowing skin.

One Serving: 190 calories; 8.25 g protein; 9.5 g total carbs; 4.5 g fiber = 5 net carbs

*Pumpkin Pie Muffin

½ C **canned pumpkin**
1 **egg**
2 T **heavy cream**
¼ C **almond flour**
1 tsp. **coconut flour**
1 tsp. **pumpkin pie spice**
½ tsp. **vanilla**
3 drops **EZ-Sweetz** (or sweetener equivalent to 1 T)
1 tsp. **baking powder**
pinch of **salt**

In ramekin: Blend pumpkin, egg, cream and vanilla.
Add dry ingredients and mix well.
Microwave   for 3 ½ to 4 minutes, or until top springs back when pressed. Immediately invert onto plate and enjoy warm, or let cool a few minutes and top with whipped cream.

*This recipe makes *two ample servings*. It is moist and rich with pumpkin and is a satisfying replacement for regular pumpkin pie over the holidays.

R egular addition of **pecans** in our diet help to decrease the LDL or "bad cholesterol" and increases HDL or "good cholesterol" levels in our blood. They are rich in monounsaturated fatty acids like oleic acid and an excellent source of age-defying antioxidants.

√**Cinnamon has long been revered as a superpower used to treat colds, indigestion, headaches and migraines, as well as stabilizing blood sugar. Just smelling cinnamon boosts memory and mental function.**

298 calories; 16 g protein; 9 g total carbs; 4 g fiber = 5 net carbs

Caramel Pecan

This recipe requires an extra mixing dish, but is well worth the effort!

2 tsp. **butter**
1 T **pecan pieces**
3 tsp. **stevia**
1 tsp. **caramel extract** *(not flavored syrup)*
¼ C **Baking Mix One**, *or*

> 2 T **almond flour**
> 4 tsp. (1 T + 1 tsp.) **vanilla whey protein**
> 2 tsp. **coconut flour**
> 1/8 tsp. (dash) **salt**
> 2/3 tsp. **baking powder**
> 1 tsp. **stevia or equivalent**

1 tsp. **cinnamon**
1 **egg**
1 T **sour cream**

Melt butter in ramekin. Add pecans, stevia and caramel extract and stir to blend.
In separate dish, combine baking mix, cinnamon, egg and sour cream and mix well.
Spoon batter over nut topping in ramekin
Microwave 1 minute 15 seconds, or until top springs back when pressed.
Put plate on top and invert, nut-side up. Spoon nuts remaining in dish onto muffin.
Guilt-free, pure delicious pleasure!

Chocolate is made by grinding the kernels of cocoa beans to a paste called chocolate liquor. Cocoa powder is made by squeezing the butter (fat) from chocolate liquor and then pulverizing it.

√The flavonoids in cocoa reduce stress and blood pressure, soothe migraines and build up body cells that are weaker in those with heart disease. Chocolate's melting point is just below your body temperature, so it melts in your mouth.

177 calories; 11 g protein; 9 g total carbs; 5.5 g fiber = 3.5 net carbs

Chocolate Muffin – Lighter Carb Version

1 **egg**
2 T **flaxseed meal**
1 T **sour cream**
1 ½ T **cocoa**
1 tsp. ***baking powder**
½ tsp. **vanilla**
3 drops **EZ Sweetz** (or equal to 3 tsp.)
  Dash of **salt**

Combine all ingredients in mug or ramekin and blend well.
*Crush or press baking powder through strainer – the little white clumps really show up if you don't.
Microwave 1 minute 15 seconds, or until top springs back when pressed.

It is wonderful enjoying this chocolate muffin knowing it is so healthful - 11 g of protein and +5 g of fiber!

L et's be honest about **whipped cream cheese**. It is a soft cheese spread that doesn't contain as much protein or calcium as other cheeses - and it is high in fat (if "low-fat" thinking still comes back to haunt).   I use it in many muffin recipes not *in addition* to cooking oils and shortenings normally used in baked goods, but *to replace them altogether*.   Two T of whipped cream cheese provides 60 calories. Two T of canola oil provides 240 calories (calories count too!) and 2 g of saturated fat, compared to 3.6 g in whipped cream cheese. So yes, it is higher in *saturated fat, but it does provide some protein and calcium along with delicious flavor.

√**The American Heart Association recommends limiting the amount of saturated fats we eat to less than 7 percent of total daily calories. For example, if we need 2,000 calories a day, that is about 16 grams of saturated fats per day.**

√ *****There is considerable debate on the pros and cons of saturated fats, with many experts agreeing that refined carbs pose a much greater danger. I believe that moderation is the key, but avoid refined sugar and hydrogenated oils whenever possible.**

333 calories; 16 g protein; 8.7 g total carbs; 3.2 g fiber = 5.5 net carbs

# Very Strawberry Shortcake

¼ C **Baking Mix One**, *or*

        2 T   **almond flour**
        4 tsp. (1 T + 1 tsp.) **vanilla whey protein**
        2 tsp.   **coconut flour**
        1/8 tsp. (dash) **salt**
        2/3 tsp. **baking powder**
        1 tsp. **stevia or equivalent**

1 tsp. dry **sugar free strawberry jello mix**
      (1/3 of small .30 box)
1 egg
1/4 cup **whipped cream cheese**, softened

In cup or ramekin: Soften cream cheese in microwave a few seconds, then thoroughly blend in egg.
Add Baking Mix and tsp. of dry strawberry jello mix and blend well Microwave 1 ½ minutes, or until top springs back when pressed.

This is rich with strawberry flavor and color, moist and delicious by itself. When cool, top with optional whipped cream.

2 tablespoons of **sour cream** have just 52 calories--half the amount of a single tablespoon of mayonnaise - and less saturated fat than a 12-ounce glass of 2% reduced fat milk, making it a delicious replacement for cooking oils

√**Sour Cream enhances immune response, balances colonic microbiota and reduces enzyme activity involved in colon irritation.**

275 calories; 14.5 g protein; 10.5 total carbs; 7.5 g fiber = 3 net carbs

 **Maple Bacon Bun**

¼ C **Baking Mix Two**, or

> 2 T **flaxseed meal**
> 1 T **almond flour**
> 1 T **coconut flour**
> 1/8 tsp. (dash) **salt**
> 2/3 tsp. **baking powder**
> 1 tsp. **stevia or equivalent**

1 **egg**
2 T **sour cream** (or 1 T sour cream and 1 T canned pumpkin)
1 tsp. **maple extract**
1 drop **EZ-Sweetz (**or sweetener equal to 1 tsp.)
1 T real **bacon bits**

Combine all ingredients in mug or ramekin until evenly blended.

Microwave 1 minute 45 seconds to 2 minutes, or until top springs back when pressed.

You will think of pancakes with warm maple syrup and bacon as you enjoy this good-for-you, breakfast-anytime muffin.

Savory
Muffins

Ricotta cheese has a sweet, nutlike flavor and can be used in both sweet and savory dishes. Ricotta literally means "recooked" in Italian. It is made from recooking the whey after it has been separated from the curds. It adds nutrient rich omega-3 fats, eliminating the need for cooking oils in many baked goods.

√An excellent source of zinc and selenium, Ricotta also boasts almost 130 milligrams of calcium per quarter cup. Its predominant nutrients include vitamin A, riboflavin and 12. vitamin B

300 calories; 17 g protein; 11 g total carbs; 8 g fiber = 3 net carbs

Ricotta Comfort Muffin

1/4 C **flaxseed meal**

1 tsp. **baking powder**

2 tsp. **stevia** or equivalent

dash of **salt**

1 **egg**

1/4 C **ricotta cheese** *or* **cream cheese**

Mix dry ingredients in mug or ramekin.

Add egg and ricotta (or cream cheese, softened) and mix well.

Microwave for 1 ½ to 2 minutes, or until top springs back when pressed.

Invert onto small plate.

This moist, buoyant muffin is wonderful for breakfast with butter and sugar-free marmalade or low-carb fruit jam.

A very nice dinner roll as well. A comfort food anytime!

Caraway seed is a popular herb used in cooking rye breads and many European dishes. Just one tablespoon is packed with a variety of B vitamins as well as vitamin C, plus a high concentration of Calcium, Iron, Magnesium, Zinc and Potassium. It has become popular for use in dietary supplements.

√In India it is common to chew <u>fennel seeds</u> after meals to facilitate digestion. The oils help facilitate proper absorption of nutrients in your stomach and intestines. They also contain anti-acidic properties. Surprisingly, they aren't really seeds at all. They're fruits!

220 calories; 7 g protein; 9.5 total carbs; 8.25 g fiber = 1.25 net carbs

Dark "Pumpernickel" Style Bread

¼ C **flaxseed meal**
1 tsp. **baking powder**
1 tsp. **stevia**
1 tsp. **cocoa**
pinch of **salt**
1 tsp. **caraway or fennel seeds** (optional)

Add:
1 **egg**
1 T **sour cream**
½ **tsp. anise extract**

Blend dry ingredients in ramekin or bun-shaped dish.
Add egg, sour cream and extract and mix well. Stir in optional seeds.
Microwave 1 minute. Invert onto plate and slice for sandwich.

Note: anise extract adds distinctive yet subtle flavor that hints of rye or pumpernickel bread. This bread is great for hearty sandwiches like reubens.

Cheddar cheese is a low carb, high-fat food, that, like everything, should be eaten in moderation. Studies have shown that diets that include cheese are associated with lower body weight as it makes you feel full longer. Consumption of dairy products also is linked to a reduced risk of developing insulin resistance syndrome.

√**Cheddar cheese, like all cheese variants, contains Conjugated Linoleic Acid (CLA) that improves insulin function and blood glucose levels. If you are lactose intolerant, many cheeses, particularly aged cheeses such as Cheddar and Swiss, contain little or no lactose and are often well tolerated.**

Large: 337 calories; 15.5 g protein; 10 g total carbs; 8.75 g fiber = 1.25 net carbs

Regular Serving: 169 calories; 7.7 g protein; 5 g total carbs; 4+ fiber = -1 net carb

*Cheese Muffin

1/4 C **flaxseed meal**
1 T **almond flour**
1/8 tsp. (dash) of **salt**
1 tsp. **baking powder**
1 tsp. **stevia** (or sweetener equal to 1 tsp.)
1 T **sour cream** (or 2 tsp. melted coconut oil)
1 **egg**
1/4 C **shredded cheddar cheese**

In mug or ramekin, add sour cream OR melted coconut oil
Add dry ingredients and blend.
Mix in 1 egg and shredded cheese until well blended.
Microwave 1 minutes if coconut oil is used; 1 ½ if sour cream is used – until top springs back when pressed.

* *Makes very large muffin, or 2 regular serving size muffins.*

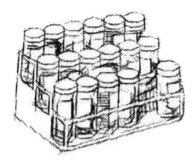

The most commonly used herbs in Italian seasoning are oregano, basil, thyme, sage, rosemary and marjoram. They are rich in antioxidants and anti-inflammatory properties. Because spices are nutrient dense, they are thermogenic, which means they naturally increase your metabolism.

√Basil, Italian spice blend's key ingredient, can protect your cells from damaging molecules that contribute to heart disease, cancer, osteoporosis and Alzheimer's disease._A tablespoon of fresh oregano has as much antioxidant power as a medium-sized apple.

175 calories; 14.5 g protein; 6.5 total carbs; 3 g fiber = 3.5 net carbs

 # Italian Herb

1 **egg**

3 T **almond flour**   (NOTE: *May use ¼ cup almond flour <u>and omit coconut flour</u>)*

1 tsp. **coconut flour**

1 T **sour cream**

1 T **Parmesan cheese**

1 tsp. **Italian seasoning**

1 tsp. **minced garlic**

1 tsp. **baking powder**

pinch **salt**

Mix all ingredients well in mug or ramekin.

Microwave approximately 50 seconds or until top springs back when pressed.

So perfect with soup or a salad.

Seeds are the "golden eggs" that contain the rich nutrients needed to nourish healthy new plants – and our bodies!. They are among the best plant sources for iron and zinc.

√**A handful of seeds a day can help you lose or maintain weight by satisfying your appetite. They can also stabilize blood-sugar levels and improve triglycerides and cholesterol, which may reduce the risk of type 2 diabetes.**

265 calories; 17.75 g protein; 11.5 g total carbs; 10 g fiber = 1.5 net carbs

# Multi-Seed Muffin

¼ C **flaxseed meal**
1 T **sunflower kernels**, roasted or raw
1 tsp. **sesame seeds**
1 tsp. **poppy seeds**
1 tsp. **baking powder**
1 tsp. **turmeric** (optional but wonderful addition.)
1 tsp. **stevia**
1 **egg**
1 T **ricotta *or* cream cheese**

Blend dry ingredients in mug or ramekin.

Add and ricotta or cream cheese and blend well.

Microwave 1 ½ minutes, or until top springs back when pressed.

I love to dip this crunchy-delicious, nutty bread in olive oil.

For breakfast, bake in a ramekin to slice and toast.   One of my favorites!

Soy flour is derived from roasted soybeans ground into a fine powder. It can be lightly "toasted" first if you desire, to enhance its nutty flavor. Put the soy flour in a dry skillet over moderate heat, stirring occasionally.

√Soy contains the antioxident *isoflavone genistein*, which helps prevent blood clots, heart attacks, strokcs and the development of artery plaques. Soybeans are the only vegetable source containing ALL essential amino acids.

One Sandwich Bun: 182 calories; 14 g protein; 7 g total carbs; 5 g fiber = 2 net carbs

Sandwich/Hamburger/Hot Dog Buns - Makes 2

1/4 C **flaxseed meal**
2 T **vanilla whey protein**
1 T **soy Flour**
1 tsp. **baking powder**
1 tsp. **stevia** or equivalent
dash of **salt**
1 egg
1/4 C **ricotta** *or* *4% milkfat small curd cottage cheese

Mix dry ingredients. Add egg and ricotta cheese and mix until well blended. Divide into two 4" ramekins for hamburger/sandwich buns and microwave, *one at a time,* for 1 minute each. A buoyant, nutty flavor, perfect for hamburger and sandwich buns.

Note: I use a microwave-safe ceramic butter dish to make hot dog buns. Minus this, if you divide the batter evenly onto two microwave-safe saucers, they will spread into flat buns. After they are baked, lightly score each down the middle (without completely cutting through) to make them easy to fold.

*Cottage cheese will not blend smooth, but the little curds create an interesting textured bread.

Soy flour provides a good protein boost. Use it to thicken gravies and cream sauces, to make homemade soymilk, or add to a variety of foods. Because it adds moisture to baked products, soy flour can also be used as an inexpensive, handy egg substitute. Replace 1 egg with 1 tablespoon soy flour and 1 tablespoon water.

√ **Soy flour is a great source of dietary fiber, iron, B vitamins and potassium. Soy also contains the nutrients magnesium and boron, which increases the effects of calcium.**

75 calories; 9 g protein; 5 g total carbs; 3.5 g fiber = 1.5 net carbs

 **Toasted Muffin**

1 T **flaxseed meal**
1 T **vanilla whey protein**
1 T **soy flour**
1 tsp. **baking powder**
2 T **water**

1 tsp. **vinegar** (regular apple cider vinegar, not white)

In ramekin, blend dry ingredients.
Add water and stir until mixed in. Batter will be thick.
Add 1 tsp. vinegar and stir until just blended. Batter will take on foamy appearance.
Microwave 1 minute, or until top springs back when pressed.
Pop out of ramekin and immediately pop into toaster.

Spread with butter (especially since no fats are in this recipe) and enjoy this crunchy muffin with your breakfast egg or smoothie.

Hippocrates, the father of medicine, used **mustard seed** medicinally. One teaspoon of white mustard seed, (the kind used in the yellow condiment) is packed with omega-3 and 6 fatty acids, potassium, phosphorous, selenium and calcium.

√Mustard seeds contain phytonutrient compounds that help prevent the risk of developing gastrointestinal cancer, magnesium to help reduce blood pressure, and components that enhance our metabolic rate.

296 calories; 12 g protein; 11 g total carbs; 7.5 g fiber = 3.5 net carbs

Deviled Egg Muffin

1/4 C **Baking Mix Two**, *or*

        2 T **flaxseed meal**
        1 T **almond flour**
        1 T **coconut flour**
        1/8 tsp. (dash) **salt**
        2/3 tsp. **baking powder**
        1 tsp. **stevia or equivalent**

1 **egg**
1 T *real* **mayonnaise** (*light* has 3.5 carbs; *real* has 0)
1 T **sugar-free sweet relish**
2 tsp. **prepared mustard**

Mix all ingredients in mug
Microwave 2 minutes, or until top springs back when pressed.

This sunny, tangy muffin has all the flavors of deviled eggs in a fraction of the time to prepare. It is delicious with chicken but is satisfying on its own.

A Tolkien Riddle: *A box without hinges, key, or lid,*
Yet golden treasure inside is hid.

Yes, the poor, misunderstood "incredible edible **egg**." According to a study by the Harvard School of Public Health, there is no significant link between egg consumption and heart disease. In fact, regular consumption of eggs may help prevent blood clots, stroke and heart attacks. In one study, women who consumed at least 6 eggs per week lowered their risk of breast cancer by 44%.

√**Every egg is not created equal. It is best to buy "cage-free" or "free-range." This means that chickens are allowed to roam, pecking what they want to eat. Research has shown that cage-free hens produce eggs that are much higher in various nutrients. Eggs from chickens fed wholesome Omega-3 foods like flaxseed are a good second choice.**

130 calories; 9.5 g protein; 1.5 total carbs; .75 g fiber = .75 net carbs

Parmesan Egg Muffin

1 T **grated parmesan cheese**
1 T **almond flour**
½ t **baking powder**
½ t **butter flavor**
 1 **egg**

Combine all ingredients in mug, mix until well blended.
Microwave 1 minute, or until top springs back when pressed.
Salt and pepper to taste.

This fluffy moist muffin can be enjoyed plain or spiced with your favorite seasoning.

A delicious variation, Parmesan Salsa Muffin, can be found on page 117.

The combination of low carbs, healthy fat and high fiber in **flax seed** make it a great food for weight loss - and maintenance. *Many dieters have discovered that flax seed is one of the most important keys to losing weight and feeling* satisfied.

√**Among all 129 of The World's Healthiest Foods, flaxseed comes out number one as a source of omega-3s. Just two tablespoons throughout a day gives you 132.9% of your daily value.**

One large muffin:
330 calories; 19 g protein; 10 g total carbs; 7 g fiber = 3 net carbs

*Savory Breakfast Muffin

1/4 C **Baking Mix Two**, or

        2 T **flaxseed meal**
        1 T **almond flour**
        1 T **coconut flour**
        1/8 tsp. (dash) **salt**
        2/3 tsp. **baking powder**
        1 tsp. **stevia or equivalent**

1 T **bacon bits**
1/4 C **shredded cheddar** (or your favorite) **cheese**
    (reserve 1 tsp.)
1 **egg**
1 T **sour cream**

In large mug or ramekin, mix all ingredients until well blended.
Batter will be thick. Sprinkle top with reserved 1 tsp. cheese.
Microwave 2 minutes or until top springs back when pressed.

*Makes a large, tasty muffin that can be divided into two servings - 19 grams of protein!

Zucchini has more potassium than a banana. The flowers of the zucchini plant are edible. Fried squash blossoms are considered a delicacy.

√**Zucchinis are rich in flavonoid poly-phenolic antioxidants such as carotenes, lutein and zea-xanthin. These compounds help scavenge harmful free-radicals from the body that play a role in aging and various diseases.**

One large serving:
227 calories; 10.5 g protein; 6.5 total carbs; 3.5 g fiber = 3 net carbs

 ***Zucchini Cheddar**

1 **egg**
1 T **coconut flour**
1 T **almond flour**
1 tsp. **baking powder**
Scant ½ tsp. **onion powder**
pinch **salt**
pinch **pepper**
¼ C **shredded zucchini, plus 1 T to set aside**
¼ C **shredded cheddar cheese**

Shred zucchini onto paper towels and lightly press out excess moisture.

Put zucchini and all other ingredients (except the 1 T of zucchini) into ramekin and mix thoroughly until well blended.

Microwave 1 ¾ to 2 minutes, or until top springs back when pressed.

Put a small dollop of sour cream on top (optional) and sprinkle with set-aside shredded zucchini.

*This makes two servings or an ample lunch.

I t takes ten pounds of milk to make one pound of **cheese**, which explains why cheese is such a concentrated source of calcium – essential for building and preserving bone health.

√**The protein in cheese can slow down the absorption of carbohydrates eaten during the same meal and therefore help balance your blood-sugar levels. The high-quality protein contained in cheese provides your body with essential building blocks for strong muscles.**

407 calories; 13.5 g protein; 10 g total carbs; 7 g fiber = 3 net carbs

Cheese Soufflé Muffin

¼ C **Baking Mix Two**, *or*

        2 T **flaxseed meal**
        1 T **almond flour**
        1 T **coconut flour**
        1/8 tsp. (dash) **salt**
        2/3 tsp. **baking powder**
        1 tsp. **stevia or equivalent**

1 T **butter**, melted
1 T **sour cream**
¼ C **shredded cheddar cheese**
1 **egg**

Microwave butter in mug or ramekin till just melted, about 15 seconds.
Add sour cream, then shredded cheese and egg, blending well.
Add baking mix and blend well.
Microwave 1 minute.
Will puff up high, then settle when removed from microwave.

Delicious, soothing comfort food. Makes a satisfying meal, especially with a side salad.

Two of the best natural sources of anti-inflammatory inhibitors are **celery** and celery seeds, which contain high amounts of painkilling apigenin. Bursitis and many other inflammatory conditions will benefit from including celery in your diet.

√ **Onions contain extraordinarily powerful compounds that are protective to the cardiovascular system, enhance immune function and fight the growth of many types of tumors. The more pungent, the more power!**

262 calories; 10 g protein; 8 g total carbs; 4 g fiber = 4 net carbs

# Stuffin' Muffin OMG Good!

1 T **butter**, melted
¼ C (slightly rounded) combination of
    chopped onions and celery
1 **egg**
1 tsp. **baking powder**
½ tsp. **poultry seasoning**
dash of **salt and pepper**
1 T **flaxseed meal**
1 T **almond flour**
1 tsp. **coconut flour**

Finely chop equal amounts of celery and onions to combine into slightly rounded ¼ cup.
Melt butter in mug or ramekin for 20 seconds in microwave.
Add chopped celery and onions and stir to coat the pieces with butter.
Cook for 1 minute. Vegetables will come out sizzling.
Add, in this order: flax meal, then almond flour, then tsp. of coconut flour, then salt and pepper, baking powder and poultry seasoning, then add egg. Mix thoroughly.
Microwave for 1 min. 15 seconds (top should spring back when pressed).
Immediately pop out onto small plate.

This muffin is unbelievably moist and rich in satisfying flavors, wonderful to accompany any holiday meal and throughout the year.

Vitamin E is often described as the "lightning rod" of the cell, deflecting damaging molecules that cause damage. This ability helps protect the skin from ultraviolet radiation. When vitamin E is applied topically, many studies show that it prevents UV damage. Vitamin E-rich foods like sunflower seeds promote this protection.

√**You get over ninety percent of the daily value for vitamin E in only a quarter cup of sunflower kernels. That same quarter-cup a day provides much of the recommended level of minerals, vitamins, phenolicanti-oxidants and protein.**

359 calories; 17 g protein; 11 g total carbs; 11 g fiber = 0 net carbs

Sesame Sun Muffin

¼ C **flaxseed meal**
1 T **sunflower kernels**
2 tsp. **sesame seeds**
1 tsp. **baking powder**
½ tsp. **turmeric**
1 tsp. **stevia or equivalent**
2 tsp. **sesame oil**
1 **egg**

Combine all ingredients in mug and mix until well blended. Microwave 1 minute or until top springs back when pressed.

A golden, nutty muffin rich in nutrients – and O net carbs!. In addition to adding beautiful orange color, Turmeric has numerous health benefits.

√**Traditional poultry seasoning mixtures contain thyme, sage, marjoram, rosemary, pepper and nutmeg.**

- It is a little-known fact that spices such as **thyme** have far greater concentrations of antioxidants than any common fruit or vegetable.

- **Sage** advice? Add it to your stews, soups and casseroles. Sage is an outstanding memory enhancer.

- Known as 'hyssop' in the Bible, **sweet marjoram** was used for purification in temples and is loaded with health benefits, including relief of cold and flu symptoms.

- Native to the Mediterranean, healthful **Rosemary** has a unique pine-like fragrance and rich pungency that summons the sea and forest.

- In the middle ages, men kept a **nutmeg** kernel in their armpit to attract admirers. It has numerous health benefits but go easy - no more than 1/2 teaspoon a day.

- **Black pepper** stimulates the taste buds and signals the stomach to increase hydrochloric acid production to improve digestion.

197 calories; 12 g protein; 9.6 total carbs; 8 g fiber = 1.6 net carbs

Fruit Stuffin' Muffin

¼ C **flaxseed meal**
¼ C **fruit substitute**: Apple or Peach
1 tsp. **baking powder**
½ tsp. **poultry seasoning**
1 **egg**
dash of **salt and pepper**

Combine dry ingredients and blend well, making sure baking powder clumps are broken down.
Add egg and fruit substitute and blend well.
Microwave 1 ½ minutes, or until top springs back when pressed.

This is a delicious change from traditional onion/celery "stuffin' " that pairs wonderfully with pork.

Note: even if you have used cinnamon in the fruit, the combination works.
Also note: Because oil was used in preparation of the fruit, no additional oil is needed in the mix.

Turmeric is a natural wonder containing curcumin, which has powerful anti-inflammatory antiviral, antibacterial and antifungal properties. Turmeric gives American yellow mustard its bright yellow color.

√Research repeatedly shows that turmeric is a powerful cancer fighter. Curcumin induces a process that triggers the self-destruction of cancerous body cells and blocks cancer growth. Sprinkle this "Queen of Spices" on eggs, chicken, soups, veggies...

282 calories; 13 g protein; 9.5 g total carbs; 7 g fiber = 2.5 net carbs

 **Savory Rich Muffin**

¼ C **Baking Mix Two**, *or*

> 2 T **flaxseed meal**
> 1 T **almond flour**
> 1 T **coconut flour**
> 1/8 tsp. (dash) **salt**
> 2/3 tsp. **baking powder**
> 1 tsp. **stevia or equivalent**

¼ C shredded **cheese** (I love shredded Italian cheese in this recipe)
1 tsp. **turmeric spice**
1 **egg**.

*In mug or ramekin, Mix all ingredients until well blended. Batter will be thick. Microwave 1 minute 30 seconds.

Delicious – and one of the most healthful things we can do for ourselves!

*You can also dollop this batter onto a microwave-safe saucer. It will spread into a nicely rounded sandwich bun.

Approximately 75 percent of **olive oil** is heart healthy monounsaturated fatty acid. Studies show that olive oil offers protection against heart disease by controlling LDL (bad) cholesterol levels, while raising HDL (good) levels.

√You can substitute one egg white plus a teaspoon of olive oil for one whole egg. Like wine, olive oil spoils if it is left in direct sunlight or if it gets too hot. Do not buy it in clear glass bottles.

320 calories; 19.5 g protein; 10.5 g total carbs; 7.25 fiber = 3.25 net carbs

# Mozzarella Yum

¼ C **Baking Mix Two,** *or*

        2 T **flaxseed meal**
        1 T **almond flour**
        1 T **coconut flour**
        1/8 tsp. (dash) **salt**
        2/3 tsp. **baking powder**
        1 tsp. **stevia or equivalent**

1 **egg**
1 tsp. **Olive Oil**
½ tsp. **Oregano** *or* **Italian Seasoning**
1 **mozzarella cheese stick**

In mug: Combine baking mix, egg, seasoning and olive oil and mix well. Cut mozzarella stick into three even pieces (easy with kitchen shears) and evenly space, cut side down, into batter until ends touch bottom of mug. Microwave 1 minute.

If you are hungry for pizza, this super-fast recipe goes a long way toward satisfying the craving. Warm stretchy cheese... savory Italian flavor...yum.

Balsamic vinegar is a thick, sweet-smelling vinegar that is made from pure and unfermented grape juice, which is known as must. It is boiled down to a thick syrup, which is then transferred to wooden barrels to age for six months to several years. The flavor is rich, complex, sweet and tangy and adds unique flavor to everything from fruit to bread, sauces and marinades.

√**To choose a nice balsamic vinegar for everyday cooking that isn't too expensive (prized Italian elixirs can cost hundreds of dollars!), look for a product that has aged in a wooden barrel for at least 3-5 years. Make sure that it does not contain any additives by checking the ingredients listed on the back of the bottle.** *Substituting sugar and regular vinegar won't work, just as tonic water and vinegar won't make champagne.*

283 calories; 14 g protein; 13 g total carbs; 4 g fiber = 9 net carbs

# Balsamic Onion Bun

¼ C **Baking Mix One**, *or*

> 2 T **almond flour**
> 4 tsp. (1 T + 1 tsp.) **vanilla whey protein**
> 2 tsp. **coconut flour**
> 1/8 tsp. (dash) **salt**
> 2/3 tsp. **baking powder**
> 1 tsp. **stevia or equivalent**

2 tsp. **butter**
¼ C thin sliced sweet **onion**
1 **egg**
1 tsp. **balsamic vinegar**

In ramekin or mug, melt butter for 20 seconds. Add onions and toss until coated with butter.   Microwave 1 minute.

Add baking mix, then egg (don't put egg directly on hot onions) and mix until egg is well blended.

Add 1 tsp. balsamic vinegar and stir until batter has foamy appearance. *Do not over-mix.*

Microwave 1 minute 15 seconds, or until top springs back when pressed.

This delicious muffin that will compliment any dinner - and will likely steal the show!

Albert Schweitzer used garlic in Africa to cure typhoid fever, typhus and cholera. In World War I it was used to prevent gangrene and in World War II, garlic was known as "Russian penicillin" because it was so effective in treating wound infections when antibiotics were not available.

√Garlic powder has all the benefits of whole garlic because it is a powdered version of whole garlic, according to the Mayo Clinic. 1/8 teaspoon is equivalent to one clove of garlic.

372 calories; 15 g protein; 6.5 total carbs; 3.25 g fiber = 3.25 net carbs

The Best Garlic Cheddar Ever

¼ C **Baking Mix One,** *or*

> 2 T **almond flour**
> 4 tsp. (1 T + 1 tsp.) **vanilla whey protein**
> 2 tsp. **coconut flour**
> 1/8 tsp. (dash) **salt**
> 2/3 tsp. **baking powder**
> 1 tsp. **stevia or equivalent**

1 T **butter**
¼ C **shredded cheddar cheese**
1 **egg**
½ to 1 tsp. **pure garlic powder (depends on how much
you love garlic)**
½ tsp. **Old Bay Seasoning**

Melt butter in mug or ramekin. Add baking mix, then all ingredients and mix until well blended.
Microwave 1 ½ to 2 minutes, or until top springs back when pressed.

This is OMG good! Wonderful with seafood, dipped in broth, whatever, whenever.

The absorption of two key carotenoid antioxidants—lycopene and beta-carotene—increases 200-400% when one cup of fresh **avocado** is added to a salad. This wonderful exotic fruit is also called the Alligator Pear, reflecting its shape and the leather-like appearance of its skin.

√**Research studies prove that the high content of monounsaturated fat in avocados is extremely beneficial to the body's metabolic system, improving weight loss results. Just one avocado contains in excess of 25 essential nutrients, including vitamins A, B, C, E, and K, copper, iron, phosphorus, magnesium - and 975 mg of potassium!**

265 calories; 15 g protein; 10 g total carbs; 6 g fiber = 4 net carbs

# Avocado Crunch Muffin

¼ C **Baking Mix One,** *or*

        2 T **almond flour**
        4 tsp. (1 T + 1 tsp.) **vanilla whey protein**
        2 tsp. **coconut flour**
        1/8 tsp. (dash) **salt**
        2/3 tsp. **baking powder**
        1 tsp. **stevia or equivalent**

2 T ripe **avocado**
1 tsp. **cinnamon**
1 tsp. **poppy seeds**
1 **egg**

In mug or ramekin, mash avocado with fork until smooth.
Add egg and blend well.
Add baking mix, poppy seeds and cinnamon and blend well.
Microwave 1 ½ to 1 ¾ minutes, or until top springs back when pressed.

Delicious, moist and crunchy. Great with a salad.

Muffin Meals

Turkey or chicken sausage is a healthier option compared to pork sausage; however, it is important to compare nutrition fact labels. You won't lose in the flavor department, with some brands brimming with herbs, spices, beets, apples and sea salt.

√Turkey sausage provides a significant number of essential vitamins and minerals, including A, C, E, B-6 and B-12. Minerals such as calcium, magnesium, phosphorus and potassium are present in high amounts.

With turkey patty, bacon bits and cheddar cheese slice:
388 calories; 25 g protein; 8 g total carbs; 4 g fiber = 4 net carbs

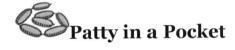Patty in a Pocket

Maple Bacon Batter Recipe:
- 1 **egg**
- 1 T **coconut flour**
- 1 T **almond flour**
- 2 T **sour cream**
  - (*or* **1T sour cream and 1T Pumpkin**)
- ¾ tsp. **baking powder**
- 1 tsp. **maple extract**
- 1 serving **stevia**
- 1 T **bacon bits** (optional)

1 **precooked turkey sausage patty or links**
1 slice of **cheddar** *or*
      American cheese (optional)

Prepare maple bacon recipe batter. Add half of batter to bottom of ramekin. Place pre-cooked (warm in microwave a few seconds) sausage patty or links and optional cheese on top of the batter. Spread remaining batter on top of sausage. Microwave 2 minutes, or until top springs back when pressed.

I've also made this without layering the batter. Mix all the ingredients in ramekin and put pre-cooked sausage or links on top. The batter will rise up around the sides and slightly over the top of the sausage as it cooks.

Option: Prepare batter in ramekin and microwave 1 ½ minutes, or until top springs back when pressed. Slice horizontally, and add desired breakfast fillings.

Dietary advice on the subject of cholesterol is often so far off that consumers compromise their health by avoiding **eggs**. According to a study by the Harvard School of Public Health, the biggest influence on blood cholesterol level is the mix of fats and carbohydrates in our diet—not the amount of cholesterol we eat from food.

√**One egg contains 6 grams of high-quality protein and all 9 essential amino acids. Because of their high sulfur content and payload of vitamins and minerals, eggs promote healthy hair and nails.**

362 calories; 19 g protein; 6.5 g carbs; 3.5 g fiber = 3 net carbs

Egg Mmmuffin

Spray 4" ramekin lightly with cooking oil, then add, in order:

1/4 C **shredded cheddar cheese**, *then*
1 slice **Canadian bacon** *or* 1Tbs **cooked bacon bits**, *then*
1 **egg** - Break yoke with fork and stir slightly without disturbing other
        ingredients, *then place*
1 tsp. (thin slice) <u>unmelted</u> **butter** on top
dash of **salt and pepper**, to your liking

For muffin - in separate dish:

1 T **vanilla whey protein**
1 T **soy flour** *or* **flaxseed meal**
1 T **almond flour**
1 tsp. **baking powder**
dash of **salt**
2 T **sour cream**

1 tsp. **coconut flour** (sprinkle this on a small saucer and set aside)

Mix dry ingredients, then add sour cream. Mix well. Batter will be very stiff. Gather with spoon into a ball, drop onto saucer with coconut flour and roll until well coated. Flatten ball into a biscuit shape (like you are making a hamburger patty), adding a bit more coconut flour if the surface is sticky. Place biscuit on top of egg/cheese ingredients in ramekin and microwave 1 1/2 minutes. Let sit in microwave 30 seconds, then invert onto small plate, egg-side up.

Yes, this is a little more trouble, but it's fun to create and the finished dish is a hearty, wholesome meal in a muffin.

Due to the lower fat content, turkey pepperoni doesn't shrink as much while cooking, allowing for more pepperoni in each bite - a big plus when satisfying a pizza craving.

√Turkey pepperoni tastes just like regular pepperoni, but with a fraction of the calories and controversial "bad" fats.   The 7 slices in this recipe contain less than 35 calories, less than 2 g total fat (most of it the good "poly" and mono") 0 trans, and 4 g of protein.

398 calories; 26.5 g protein; 10 g total carbs; 4 g fiber = 6 net carbs

# Pizza Muffin

Italian Herb Muffin Recipe:
1 **egg**
3 T **almond flour** (*May Use ¼ cup almond flour and omit coconut flour*)
1 tsp. **coconut flour**
1 T **sour cream**
1-2 T **Parmesan cheese**
1 tsp. **Italian seasoning**
1 tsp. **minced garlic**
1 tsp. **baking powder**
pinch of **salt**

2 T **Italian-style tomato sauce** (or your favorite low carb marinara)
1 T chopped **onion**
1T chopped **green pepper**
7 slices **turkey pepperoni**
¼ C **shredded mozzarella**

Prepare Italian -style muffin recipe. Spread half of batter in bottom of ramekin. Drizzle on 1 T tomato sauce. Layer the onions, green pepper, mozzarella, pepperoni and the remaining tomato sauce. Spoon remaining batter over all. Microwave for approximately 2 minutes 30 seconds. Center might still be damp. Let stand 2-3 minutes to complete cooking. Transfer to plate if desired. So-o-o good!

Note: Substitute your favorite pizza toppings as your plan allows.

Cabbage becomes a super-food when it is pickled. The fermentation process produces a substance called isothiocynates, which prevent cancer growth. The American Center for Cancer Research has found that sauerkraut has a profound effect in preventing and healing breast cancer.

√Sauerkraut has been used as an immune booster for centuries. It contains phytochemicals which combat numerous common ills including the common cold, skin problems, and weight gain. Captain James Cook circumnavigated the globe without losing a single crewmember to scurvy (vitamin C deficiency) thanks to the foods his ship carried, including sixty barrels of sauerkraut.

420 calories; 21 g protein; 14.75 total carbs; 9.25 g fiber = 5.5 net carbs

# Reuben Muffin Meal

In separate bowl, mix recipe for Dark Pumpernickel Style Bread:

¼ C **flaxseed meal**
1 tsp. **baking powder**
1 tsp. **stevia**
1 tsp. **cocoa**
pinch of **salt**
1 tsp. **caraway or fennel seeds** (optional)
1 **egg**
1 T **sour cream**
1/2 tsp. **anise extract**

Filling:
1 slice **swiss cheese**
¼ C **sauerkraut** with excess moisture pressed out
3 thin slices (1 oz.) **corned beef**
2-3 tsp. **1000 island dressing** *or* **mustard**

• Blend dry ingredients in ramekin or bun-shaped dish. Add egg, sour cream and extract and mix well. Stir in optional seeds.
• Place 1/2 batter in 4 " ramekin and sprinkle cheese on top, then sauerkraut (excess moisture pressed out with paper towels) over that, then squiggle on mustard or thousand island dressing, then corned beef slices.
• Dollop remaining half of batter on top.
• Microwave approx. 2 minutes, or until top springs back when pressed. Immediately invert onto small plate.

Makes large hearty sandwich with flavors wonderfully blended.

The Food and Drug Administration (FDA) and the Environmental Protection Agency (EPA) are advising women who may become pregnant, pregnant women, nursing mothers, and young children to avoid some types of fish and eat fish and shellfish that are lower in mercury.

The National Resources Defense Council created the chart below as a guideline to how much tuna can be eaten by children, pregnant women or women wanting to conceive, based on their weight.

Weight in Pounds	Frequency	
	White Albacore	**Chunk Light**
20lbs	1 can/10 wks	1 can/3 wks
30lbs	1 can/6 wks	1 can/2 wks
40lbs	1 can/5 weeks	1 can/11 days
50lbs	1 can/4 weeks	1 can/9 days
60lbs	1 can/3 weeks	1 can/7 days
70lbs	1 can/3 weeks	1 can/6 days
80lbs	1 can/2 weeks	1 can/ 6 days
90lbs	1 can/2 weeks	1 can/5 days
100lbs	1 can/2 weeks	1 can/5 days
110lbs	1 can/12 days	1 can/4 days
120lbs	1 can/11 days	1 can/4 days
130lbs	1 can/10 days	1 can/4 days
140lbs	1 can/10 days	1 can/3 days
150lbs +	1 can/9 days	1 can/3 days

Source: Food and Drug Administration test results for mercury and fish, and the Environmental Protection Agency's determination of safe levels of mercury.

 # Tuna Melt

1 pouch **light tuna in water,** 2.5 oz. single serving size
1 T diced **onion**
1 T diced **celery** (about a 2" section of stalk)
½ tsp. **dill weed**
2 T **flaxseed meal**
1 tsp. **baking powder**
dash of **salt and pepper**
1 **egg**
*1 **cheddar cheese stick**

In ramekin, combine all ingredients *except cheese stick* until well blended.
Cut cheese stick into four pieces and evenly space into batter until cut ends touch bottom.
Microwave 2 minutes 15 seconds to 2 ½ minutes, until top (between areas of melted cheese) spring back when pressed. Remove to serving plate and "frost" with dollop of mayonnaise or sour cream, if desired. The celery and onion will be warm and crunchy.

* If you prefer, fold in ¼ C of shredded cheese instead. I prefer the cheese stick method to enjoy pockets of melted cheese, rather than blended throughout.

309 calories; 32 g protein; 6 g total carbs; 5.50 g fiber = .5 net carbs

A hot dog can contain between one-quarter and one-third of the 2,300 mg of sodium you need for an entire day. A beef hot dog has a "ballpark" (couldn't pass up the pun) figure of 600 mg; pork has 620. Low-fat hot dogs can have the most sodium with over 700 mg per serving, and a lot more sugar. The brand I use, Applegate Farms Uncured Turkey Hot Dogs, has 260 mg. of sodium, 3 g total fat, 0 carbs, and 5 g of protein.

√**It is especially important to read labels and compare brands. Some turkey frankfurters also contain beef, or casings that contain gluten, corn syrup and ingredients you can't pronounce. (If it says "mechanically separated turkey," look it up to see what that means!)**

355 calories; 22 g protein; 10 g total carbs; 7 g fiber = 3 net carbs

 Muffin Dog

¼ C **Baking Mix Two**, or

> 2 T **flaxseed meal**
> 1 T **almond flour**
> 1 T **coconut flour**
> 1/8 tsp. (dash) **salt**
> 2/3 tsp. **baking powder**
> 1 tsp. **stevia or equivalent**

1 **turkey frankfurter**
1 **cheese stick**, any kind
1 **egg**
1 T **sour cream**

Warm frankfurter in microwave 15 seconds to remove refrigerator chill and bring to slightly above room temperature. Cut exactly in half (not lengthwise).
In mug: Combine baking mix, egg and sour cream and mix well.
Cut cheese stick in half and combine with frankfurter halves to make a bundle.
Insert into center of batter, cut-sides down, until it touches bottom of mug.
Microwave 1 minute and 45 seconds. Batter will rise up around "dog" until only tips are showing. Test top of batter for doneness (may require a few more seconds), then remove immediately onto plate.

You can cut the sandwich in half, between the frank halves, to add your favorite hot-dog condiments. I usually use a paper cupcake liner or coffee filter to hold it and dip in mustard.
Cheese is a wonderful addition when "baked" all together.

Salsa is Spanish for sauce and traditionally contains a combination of tomatoes, onions, cilantro and spice from chili peppers – each packed with powerful nutrients. It is very low in saturated fat and cholesterol and a good source of vitamins, magnesium, phosphorus, fiber, potassium, copper and manganese. If you make salsa at home you can eliminate the one bad thing about most commercial brands: way too much sodium.

√In low-carbohydrate diets, salsa is a zesty addition to dishes because it contains an average of 10 calories per serving (1 g of carbohydrates). It has surpassed ketchup in America in popularity.

135 calories; 4 g protein; 2.50 total carbs; 1.25 g fiber = 1.25 net carbs

Parmesan Salsa Muffin

1 T grated **parmesan**
1 T **almond flour**
1/2 tsp. **baking powder**
1 **egg**
1 T **salsa**, rounded

Mix all ingredients in mug until well blended.
Microwave 1 minute.

Moist, flavorful and delicious - a very nice breakfast or light lunch meal.

Crab meat is carbohydrate free, making it a great diet food if you are trying to lose weight, build muscles or have diabetes. It is rich in chromium, which helps insulin to metabolize sugar and thereby lower blood glucose levels.

√All shellfish have plentiful amounts of selenium, an antioxidant that cancels out the carcinogenic effects of cadmium, mercury and arsenic, which cause tumors. In addition to being high in vitamins, high-quality proteins and amino acids, crab meat is rich in calcium, copper, zinc, phosphorus and iron. Another plus? Crabs contain sterol, which restricts the absorption of cholesterol in other foods eaten during a meal.

360 calories; 28.5 g protein; 8 g total carbs; 3 g fiber = 5 net carbs

Mozzarella *Crab Muffin *Can Substitute Cooked Chicken

¼ C **Baking Mix One,** *or*

> 2 T **almond flour**
> 4 tsp. (1 T + 1 tsp.) **vanilla whey protein**
> 2 tsp. **coconut flour**
> 1/8 tsp. (dash) **salt**
> 2/3 tsp. **baking powder**
> 1 tsp. **stevia or equivalent**

¼ C **crabmeat** (*or* cooked **chicken**), chopped
¼ C shredded **mozzarella cheese**
1 T chopped **chives,** dried or fresh
2 T **sour cream**
1 **egg**
¼ tsp. **dry mustard**
  Dash of **pepper**

Thoroughly mix all ingredients in ramekin until well blended.
Microwave 2 ½ minutes, or until top springs back when pressed.

Note: A side salad would complete a delicious full meal.

R ead labels on the back of taco seasoning packets. Too many contain ingredients like maltodextrin (sugar), corn starch (corn), yellow corn flour (corn) monosodium glutamate (MSG), high amounts of sodium and ethoxyquin, which is used both as a preservative *and* a pesticide! If you can't find organic brands that contain just spices, you can easily make your own and adjust it to your taste.

Taco Seasoning

4 T **chili powder**

1 tsp. **garlic powder**

1 tsp. **onion powder**

1 tsp. **cayenne pepper**

1 tsp. **oregano**

2 tsp. **paprika**

2 T **cumin powder**

2 tsp. **sea salt**

2 tsp. **ground black pepper**

√**Capsaicin, the hot pepper's natural heat-causing component, has been proven to kill cancer cells, promote fat oxidation, prevent sinus infections, provide gastric relief and serve as an anti-inflammatory agent that eases arthritic swelling and pain.**

435 calories; 24.5 g protein; 7 g total carbs; 3.25 g fiber – 3.75 net carbs

# Southwest Cheese Muffin

¼ C **Baking Mix One**

>2 T **almond flour**
>4 tsp. (1 T + 1 tsp.) **vanilla whey protein**
>2 tsp. **coconut flour**
>1/8 tsp. (dash) **salt**
>2/3 tsp. **baking powder**
>1 tsp. **stevia or equivalent**

1 **egg**
1 tsp. **taco seasoning**
1 tsp. **olive oil**
Optional: Add a few drops of hot sauce
 2 **cheddar cheese sticks**
Dollop of **sour cream** *(optional)*

In ramekin, combine baking mix, egg, seasoning and olive oil. Mix until egg is well blended. Batter will be thick. Smooth evenly in bottom of ramekin.
Cut each cheese stick into 3 even pieces with kitchen shears. Space the 6 cheese pieces into batter, cut-side down, until each touches bottom of ramekin.
Microwave 1 minute, or until top springs back when pressed. You may need to microwave an additional 15 seconds.
Transfer to serving dish and if desired, top with dollop of sour cream. This is a delicious, savory meal.

As tiny as they are, caraway seeds are beneficial in huge ways, from regulating stomach functions, inhibiting gas formation and bloating, to strengthening the body's immune system and alleviating cold symptoms.

√In the British Isles, caraway was once thought to prevent fickleness and keep things from straying or getting lost. Whether a spouse or a chicken, neither would end up in the wrong bed or roost after a rub-down with caraway. In many places around the world it is still sometimes given to homing pigeons - or slipped into breakfast toast.

238 calories; 19.5 g protein; 6.75 g total carbs; 4.50 g fiber = 2.25 net carbs

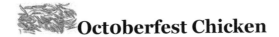

Octoberfest Chicken

¼ C diced **chicken**
¼ C **sauerkraut,** excess moisture pressed out
½ tsp. **garlic powder**
½ tsp. **onion powder**
1 tsp. **paprika**
½ tsp. **caraway seeds (optional)**
2 T **flaxseed meal**
1 tsp. **baking powder**
1 **egg**
Dash of **pepper and salt**
1 ½ T **sour cream** (set aside)

Squeeze excess moisture from sauerkraut between paper towels.
In ramekin, combine flaxseed meal, egg, baking powder and seasonings
and mix well. Stir in chicken, sauerkraut and optional caraway seeds until
evenly blended throughout.

Microwave 2 ¼ - 2 ½ minutes. If quarter-sized spot in middle is still very
slightly damp, it will finish cooking when inverted onto plate.
"Frost" with sour cream.

Index

15447773R00076

Made in the USA
San Bernardino, CA
25 September 2014